# Emerald's Journal

## ~ a summer with hatchlings

by pamela s. allison

 sand sage press * canyon, tx * usa * earth

Sand Sage Press

Canyon, Texas

www.SandSagePress.com

photographs by Joseph C. Cepeda

Printed on recycled paper with soy ink in South Korea.


Allison, Pamela S.

  Emerald's Journal : a summer with hatchlings / Pamela S. Allison

  1st ed.

  Summary:  a girl records in her journal her summer experiences with the hatching of horned toads.

  Includes scientific journal (p)

  Includes additional resources (p v)

  ISBN 978-0-9793474-1-2  (hardcover : alk. paper)

  1. Horned toads—West (U.S.)   2. Texas Horned Lizard—West (U.S.)   3. Reptiles—West (U.S.)

  I. Allison, Pamela S. journalist.   II. Cepeda, Joseph C. photographer.   III. Title

597.95 – dc22

Library of Congress Control Number:  2007925782

# Acknowledgments

On behalf of horned lizards, I must express appreciation to the Horned Lizard Conservation Society for providing a forum for information; the many biologists that have contributed to the body of knowledge about horned lizards; and especially to Wendy Hodges and Wade Sherbrooke who generously share their insight and knowledge gained over decades of studying horned lizards.

Finally, I express my appreciation
to Joe, for sharing these events,
to Emerald, whose love and caring nature continues
        to inspire her family,
to Scott, Christee, Daniel, and Holly for enriching
        my life,
and to each of my grandchildren and the future
generations of scientists, in whom I see hope
        for other creatures,
        for dreaming what is possible, and
        for having the courage to make it so.

# Additional Information About Horned Lizards

The definitive work about the 13 species of horned lizards in western North America, 5 of which are found only in Mexico, is:

Sherbrooke, Wade C. 2003. Introduction to Horned Lizards of North America. University of California Press, Berkeley.

The national organization devoted to educating about and conserving horned lizards publishes a quarterly newsletter Phrynosomatics and, when possible, funds small grants to benefit the future of horned lizards. For membership or to request information about horned lizards, contact:

Horned Lizard Conservation Society
PO Box 122
Austin, Texas 78767
www.hornedlizards.org

v

# Introduction

This journal is rooted in a lifelong love for horned lizards – you may know them as horny toads or, even, horned frogs. Many of you share this love! It is a story that began long before turf grass, sprinkler systems, and "anticides" became the norm.

Sadly, today, there are too few opportunities
for children to develop a relationship with this gentle creature.

Texas Horned Lizards ( *Phrynosoma cornutum* ) are protected as a "threatened" species in Texas. Although its common name includes the descriptor "Texas," the majority of its home range – in addition to Texas – includes Oklahoma and parts of Kansas, Colorado, New Mexico, Arizona, and much of Mexico.

This journal is written from the viewpoint of a 7-year old girl, and based on events in the natural world that have enriched our lives and inspired this journal. Pam sent the birth announcement that follows to family and friends, and the intellectual and scientific adventure was on.

Emerald's journal includes real data gathered by the author through observations and studies of horned lizards. The scientific studies reported herein were conducted in accordance with a scientific permit issued by the Texas Parks and Wildlife Department and no horned lizards were harmed.

The "eruption" of tiny, energetic horned lizards was an event that transformed our summer. We hope Emerald's Journal will allow us to share this experience with you.

to horned lizards everywhere
and
to children of all ages
that love them enough
to let them

be

# It's a Boy! and a Girl! and... birth announcement!

Conception culminated in the construction of a nest on the eve of May 25 with an unknown number of eggs laid to incubate.

Births occurred on the eve of July 25 in celebration of Holly's birthday... at which time the nintuplets (maybe more) dug their escape hatch and began their above-ground journey under the cover of darkness...

Interestingly enough, both eventful dates coincided with the New Moon.

The first of the nintuplets was discovered 16 inches from the escape hatch, having buried itself in shallow soil with only her head exposed (appearing curiously as a rock). The photographic journey of the births began!

Each of the 9 babies measured in at about 1-inch in length, but weighed in at too-small to register on my scale...

All appear healthy and well on their way to their place in the sun... (in preparation for which, I have tolerated way too-many ant bites this year)!

26 July, one summer

My Journal

# my horny toad journal
## by Emerald

the horny toad dug her ~~next~~ nest here.

there is bare dirt to run on and plants to hide under.

And Ants! ants! ants!

# horny toads are really Lizards

not toads.

uh-oh!

this is a male horny Toad.
Scientists use symbols For short.
♂ means male. He is waiting
for ants.
♀ is for females

horny toads hide from their ~~enemies~~
enemies. Or try to escape.
Or sit very still.
Or puff up
to
look scary!

My Memaw said
they can spit blood from their
eyes.
Scary!!!

There are different kinds of horny toads.
Some kinds lay eggs.

These
♀s
are
soo-o
beautiful.

After
laying
eggs,
she
looked
all
shriveled
up.

♀ before laying
eggs – 45 grams

♀ after eggs weighed
25 grams

# the nest

the ♀ is digging her nest. For her eggs.

"are you watching me?"

is she laying an egg?→

she covered the nest.
←Before the camoflage
after↓

there was a blue rubber band by the nest. She broke it into little pieces, for camoflag.

the big day

← escape hole

the **1st** hatchling

I can't believe it is so little.

# the hatchlings weighed

0.74 grams
0.81 "
0.75 "
0.68 "
0.66 "
0.71 "
0.57 "

a penny weighs 2.50 grams

# how to measure horny toads

with a ruler

nose to end
of its tail

and

nose to vent
*help!* (the vent is
by its tail upside
down)

2 days old hatchlings

bury for the night

big red ants for big horny toads to eat.

little tiny ants for **baby** and teenager horny toads. to eat. We need more ants!

"uh-oh. My lunch is on my head!"

Animal poop is called SCAT !

Baby horny toad scat is ~~itsy-bitsy~~ like this.

# If horny toads find lots of ants, they grow!

hatchlings

Shed their skin sometimes.

1 month old weighed 1.82 grams

1 day old 0.74 grams

# My pictures of

horny toads

I ♡ horny toads

and
ants

From Emerald